It Won't Last Forever

*With love, respect, and gratitude,
this book is dedicated to
MIKE BURCH—
from your No. 1 fan,
your mother-in-law.*

The hardest thing about having a sad mother was that Kristen worried so much. She used to believe that her mother would always be strong and brave and able to take care of her and her new baby brother. She knew they couldn't possibly take care of themselves.

Her mother spent hours each day lying on the couch in her nightgown with a blanket wrapped around her. Kristen just didn't know how to make her mom smile anymore. And ever since her mother lost her job and her dad moved out, her mom cried for hours every day. She didn't talk to her friends, didn't eat very much, and didn't seem interested in what happened to Kristen.

Kristen came home right after school to help take care of her little brother. She didn't like having to grow up so fast!

While her mother went job-hunting, Mrs. Gerhart, a lady who lived next door, took care of Kristen and her little brother. Kristen was glad when Mrs. G said, "You can go down to the pool every day after school. I'll be glad to watch the baby without your help for another hour. You need some time to play." Her special friend Barbara was the Activities Director, and she DID want to talk to her. Barbara was alone with Kristen when Kristen asked, "What's the matter with my mom, anyway?"

Barbara said, "Your mother has a sickness called depression. It's her illness that makes her not want to talk or enjoy watching you participate in a swimming meet. She may not know that depression is a treatable problem.

"I know that at first you thought it was wonderful that she wasn't telling you what to do all of the time, but now you know it's scary when an adult is not in charge."

Kristen hung her head and whispered, "Once, when I was making loud noises with my straw at the table, my mother said, "You are driving me crazy."

Barbara put her arm around Kristen and in the kindest voice said, "Children never have the power to make their parents sick or to make them well. Besides, I know that your mother had a depression once before you were even born."

It felt good to have Barbara hug her and be so kind. Kristen couldn't keep back the tears any longer and blurted out, "The teacher asked questions about my mother today in front of the class, and I was so embarrassed."

Barbara said, "I'm glad you are telling me how you feel. Trying NOT to feel angry or worried will use up all of your energy and make it hard for you to concentrate at school."

When she finished swimming, Kristen hurried back to her family's condo. When she entered the living room, her mother yelled, "Don't you know that I need you to help me?"

Kristen screamed back, "You don't care about me.

All you care about is yourself. Why did you get depressed, anyway?"

Kristen left the room to take care of her brother. While she sat on the rug playing with him, she let the tears run down her face. Grandma had said she should be strong and not cry. Kristen decided Grandma was wrong. Some things *are* worth crying about!

She went to the bathroom to wipe her face, and that's when she saw the new bottle of sleeping pills. *Mom wouldn't try to kill herself, would she?* Kristen wondered. She even thought about hiding the pills.

The next day when she came home from school, there was a paramedic truck in front of their condominium building. Kristen's heart pounded so hard that she thought it would explode. When she got home, Mrs. G was standing there holding her brother and said, "Your mother will be fine. There is nothing to worry about." But since the paramedics had taken her mother away, she felt sure Mrs. G was just trying to protect her from the truth.

Kristen ran to the window and watched the truck pull away. "How could you do such a stupid thing? DON'T YOU DARE DIE!" She sat on the couch and cried and cried. Soon she felt Barbara's arms wrapped around her. Kristen leaned on her shoulder and said, "They didn't give me a chance to say good-bye. I could have told her how much I loved her, and that I was sorry I yelled at her last night."

"Dear Kristen, being angry is normal when a child has a depressed parent. Your mother didn't try to hurt herself because of you. . . What else are you worrying about?" Kristen said she wanted someone to tell her exactly what had happened, and Barbara said, "Yes, you have a right to know. Let's ask Mrs. G."

Mrs. G said she had found Kristen's mother lying on the floor with the empty pill bottle beside her, and that she had called the paramedics. Kristen's mom had left a note that said, "Take good care of my kids. They will be better off without me."

Kristen knew her mother was VERY wrong—they

WOULDN'T be better off without her. She was glad the doctor would make her mother well again; at least she HOPED he would. Mrs. G said Kristen and her brother could stay with her family until her mother could take care of them again. "Now, Kristen, why don't you go down to the pool with Barbara for a while and play."

On the way to the pool, Barbara said, "What happened is awful and I know how scared you are, but I want you to know that you will never ever be alone. Lots of people love you and will take care of you while your mother is sick."

That night at the dinner table, Kristen hit Angela, Mrs. G's little girl. And Angela hit her back. Mrs. G said, "Kristen, you are fighting so that you can end up crying. But you're not crying about the fighting, you're crying because you are worried about your mother. You don't have to fight to cry about that . . . it's okay to cry about being worried."

Her mother had been in the hospital for two weeks, and finally Kristen had permission to come and visit her. Barbara would go with her. Kristen was scared and excited at the same time. The door was locked to the part of the hospital where her mother was staying. While they were standing by the door, they met the doctor who was taking care of her mother. Barbara said he was a psychiatrist, a doctor who helps people understand their feelings.

The doctor looked at Barbara and said, "It's good that you came in the afternoon when she is feeling more awake after her treatment." He never looked at Kristen. Kristen spoke up and said, "I'm her daughter and I want to know how to help my mom."

The doctor said:
1. You can paint a picture for her wall.
2. You can ask her advice about something so she feels like a mother still.
3. And you can tell her that you love her.

After three weeks, her mother told Kristen she would be coming home from the hospital. Kristen was surprised by how she felt. First she felt relieved, and then she felt really mad. Now that her mother was better, all of the frightened feelings were coming to the surface of her mind. Her feelings didn't make sense until Barbara said, "Feelings don't HAVE to make sense. Feelings just ARE."

When her mother was home, she told Kristen that she would be taking medication, reading helpful books, taking long walks every day, and talking to her friends. She said that the medicine made her have a dry mouth and feel sleepy sometimes. The most important thing for Kristen to know was that her mother had a psychiatrist now who was her "worry doctor," and that she could talk to him about her feelings. She said, "YOU don't have to take care of me."

Kristen was glad to know that they would have Easter dinner at Mrs. G's house, and that Mrs. G was making homemade noodles. After dinner, all of the kids who lived at the condos would get together for the Easter egg hunt. She could hardly wait. Kristen was sure the Easter bunny wasn't "for real," but it was still fun to sit on the grass and wait for the big chocolate egg from the giant bunny.

When the other kids went home, Kristen sat alone. Next thing she knew, there was Barbara in the bunny costume, sitting next to her. Kristen said, "No WONDER I liked the Easter bunny!" and they both laughed and rolled on the grass. It felt good to laugh. She said, "Barbara, I asked my mom if she got sick because of me and she said no, that she probably would have been MORE depressed if she didn't love me and my brother so much!" Barbara just smiled and gave her a hug.

Kristen had learned so much since her mother became ill. She learned that she never needed to be ashamed of her feelings, and that it was her actions that were really important. She learned that she could find people to talk to when she needed to talk, and she learned that having a sick mother was hard, but not the end of the world.

Most important of
all, she learned that
she could deal with
her problems . . . with
a little help from
her friends.

Dear Friend,

The child who lives with a depressed parent is also suffering. Here are some guidelines for helping the child.

1. Children may assume blame for the parent's illness and must be told that they could not cause an emotional illness.

2. Children may have lowered self-esteem due to lack of affirmation and because they are sometimes the recipients of their parent's anger. Focused attention will help offset this.

3. Children need nurture, warmth, and to have fun with other caring adults.

4. Tell the child that the depressed parent can't make the sad feelings go away without help, but the depression won't last forever, either.

5. Children should be invited to ask any questions they choose, and they should be given honest answers about anti-depressant medication, electro-convulsive therapy, psychiatric hospitals, psychologists and psychiatrists, and suicide attempts.